BIGGEST NAMES IN SPORTS
MATTHEW STAFFORD
FOOTBALL STAR

by Matt Scheff

FOCUS READERS

NAVIGATOR

WWW.FOCUSREADERS.COM

Focus Readers is distributed by North Star Editions:
sales@northstareditions.com | 888-417-0195

Produced for Focus Readers by Red Line Editorial.

Library of Congress Cataloging-in-Publication Data
Library of Congress Cataloging-in-Publication Data is available on the Library of Congress website.

ISBN
978-1-63739-442-7 (hardcover)
978-1-63739-443-4 (paperback)
978-1-63739-445-8 (ebook pdf)
978-1-63739-444-1 (hosted ebook)

Printed in the United States of America
Mankato, MN
082022

ABOUT THE AUTHOR

Matt Scheff is an author and artist living in Alaska. He enjoys mountain climbing, fishing, and curling up with his two Siberian huskies to watch sports.

TABLE OF CONTENTS

CHAPTER 1

SUPER BOWL CHAMPION

The Los Angeles Rams were struggling. And it was happening at the worst possible time. The Rams were playing the Cincinnati Bengals in the Super Bowl. Earlier in the game, the Rams had lost several key players to injury. In the second half, the Bengals had taken a 20–16 lead.

Matthew Stafford looks for an open receiver during the Super Bowl.

Only six minutes remained in the game. Rams quarterback Matthew Stafford led his offense onto the field. Los Angeles needed a touchdown. The Super Bowl rested on Stafford's right arm.

Until 2021, Stafford had spent his entire career with the Detroit Lions. During that time, the Lions had never won a playoff game. Stafford had little experience in pressure-packed situations. The crowd roared, wondering if he could come up big at such an important time.

The Bengals defense was built to stop big plays. So, Stafford attacked with quick, short passes. Most of them went to his favorite receiver, Cooper Kupp.

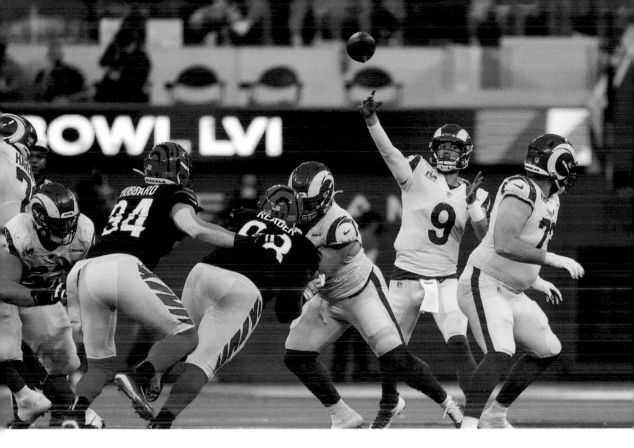

Stafford heaves a pass against the Cincinnati Bengals in Super Bowl LVI.

Stafford and the Rams marched down the field bit by bit. On one play, Stafford looked to his right. But then he threw the ball to Kupp on his left. The stunning no-look pass went for 22 yards. It was the longest play of the drive.

With 1:44 left to play, the Rams were at Cincinnati's 4-yard line. Stafford zipped a pass to Kupp in the end zone. However, a holding penalty erased the touchdown. Stafford would have to do it again.

On the 15th play of the long drive, Stafford took the snap. He dropped back and turned to his right. Kupp faked a move to his inside and then ran toward the sideline. Stafford lofted a perfect throw. Kupp snatched the ball out of the air just before a defender could push him out of bounds. It was a touchdown! The Rams took the lead, 23–20.

The Bengals failed on their final drive, and the Rams stormed onto the field.

Stafford tosses the winning touchdown pass to Cooper Kupp in the Super Bowl.

After years of losing with the Lions, Stafford was at the top of the football world. He was a Super Bowl champion.

CHAPTER 2

EARLY YEARS

John Matthew Stafford was born on February 7, 1988. As a kid, Matthew was a great athlete. He played soccer, basketball, baseball, and more. But the football field was where he really excelled.

Matthew played quarterback for Highland Park High School in University Park, Texas. In 2005, he led the team to a

Matthew Stafford drops back to pass during a 2006 game with the Georgia Bulldogs.

perfect 15–0 record. Best of all, the team won a state championship. Matthew's strong, accurate arm made him a hot **prospect**. Colleges around the country wanted Matthew to play for them.

FAMOUS FRIEND

One of Stafford's childhood friends was Clayton Kershaw. Kershaw was a star pitcher for their school's baseball team. He also played center on the football team. Kershaw went on to huge success in Major League Baseball. He won three Cy Young Awards as the National League's best pitcher. He also won the league's Most Valuable Player Award in 2014. Stafford and Kershaw remained friends. They cheered for each other as professionals.

Stafford scrambles during a rainy game at Auburn in 2006.

Stafford was eager to start his college career. In 2006, he graduated from high school a few months early. He attended the University of Georgia. Stafford began the 2006 season as the Bulldogs' **backup** quarterback. But in the third game,

Georgia's **starter** got injured. Stafford stepped in.

It was a rough start. At one point, the Bulldogs lost four out of five games. However, they came on strong later in the season. Stafford led Georgia to a huge **upset** of No. 5 Auburn. The Bulldogs went on to play in the Chick-fil-A Bowl. In that game, Stafford led a big second-half comeback. Georgia defeated Virginia Tech 31–24.

Stafford kept improving. In 2007, he led Georgia to an impressive 11–2 record. And in 2008, he took an even bigger step forward. His 25 touchdown passes were the most ever thrown by a Georgia

Stafford rolls out of the pocket during a 2008 game against Central Michigan.

quarterback. Stafford led the Bulldogs all the way to the Capital One Bowl.

Stafford was at his best in that game. He threw three touchdown passes in the second half. Georgia beat Michigan State 24–12. It ended up being the last game of Stafford's college career.

CHAPTER 3

LEADING THE LIONS

Matthew Stafford decided to leave Georgia after his junior season. He was ready to take the next step. He entered the 2009 National Football League (NFL) **Draft**. Stafford had all the tools NFL teams wanted to see in a quarterback. He was big, strong, and **durable**. The Detroit Lions chose Stafford

Stafford (right) displays his jersey after being drafted by the Detroit Lions.

with the first pick in the draft. Fans in Detroit hoped Stafford would help end years of losing.

Stafford struggled as a **rookie**. He threw three interceptions in his first game. In his second game, Stafford threw his first NFL touchdown pass. He hit star receiver Calvin Johnson with an eight-yard pass. It was the start of a great partnership with Johnson.

Stafford dealt with injuries in 2009 and 2010. But he was healthy in 2011. That year, Stafford threw for more than 5,000 yards. He was just the fourth quarterback in NFL history to do so. Stafford also helped Detroit reach the

Stafford congratulates Calvin Johnson after a touchdown in 2011.

playoffs for the first time in years. The Lions faced the New Orleans Saints. Stafford tossed three touchdown passes in the game. However, Detroit's defense couldn't stop the Saints. New Orleans won 45–28.

Much of Stafford's career in Detroit followed that same pattern. Year after year, he put up huge passing numbers. But the Lions rarely made the playoffs. And when they did, they always lost in the first round.

HEALTH SCARE

Stafford married Kelly Hall in 2015. The couple started a family, welcoming three daughters. But the Staffords got a big scare in 2019. Doctors found a **tumor** in Kelly's brain. She went through a 12-hour surgery to remove it. Stafford took some time off from the Lions to be there for Kelly and the girls. Kelly recovered, and the Staffords welcomed a fourth daughter in 2020.

Stafford fires a pass in a 2018 game against the Green Bay Packers.

From 2011 to 2019, Stafford started 136 straight games. That was the sixth-longest streak for a quarterback in NFL history. It finally ended in 2019. Stafford injured his back. He played in only eight games that season. Some fans began to wonder if Stafford's best days were behind him.

CHAPTER 4

MOVING WEST

Matthew Stafford was back on the field for Detroit in 2020. It was another bad season for the Lions. The team went 5–11 and missed the playoffs. A few months later, the Lions traded Stafford to the Los Angeles Rams. The Rams had a loaded **roster**. They hoped Stafford was the final piece to their Super Bowl puzzle.

Stafford warms up before his first game with the Los Angeles Rams.

Stafford quickly formed a bond with receiver Cooper Kupp. And the team's offense proved to be a powerful force. Los Angeles surged to a 7–1 start. The Rams finished with a 12–5 record and earned a spot in the playoffs.

In the first round, the Rams easily beat the Arizona Cardinals. Next, the Rams faced the Tampa Bay Buccaneers. The game was a classic. Stafford led an offensive explosion. Los Angeles built a 27–3 lead in the third quarter. However, the Bucs charged back to tie the game with just 42 seconds to go.

Stafford didn't have much time. But he got to work. He connected with Kupp on a

Stafford squares off against his old team in Week 7 of the 2021 season.

20-yard pass. On the next play, Stafford launched a deep throw to Kupp. The 44-yard play set up a game-winning field goal. The Rams had survived Tampa Bay's furious comeback.

In the next game, it was Stafford's turn to lead a comeback. The Rams trailed the San Francisco 49ers 17–7 in the fourth quarter. Stafford zipped a touchdown pass to Kupp to cut into the lead. Then he led two late field-goal drives. Kicker Matt Gay booted the game-winner with less than two minutes to play.

RECEIVER'S BEST FRIEND

In 2012, Lions receiver Calvin Johnson set an NFL record. That year, he racked up 1,964 receiving yards. In 2021, Rams receiver Cooper Kupp nearly beat Johnson's mark. He fell just short, gaining 1,947 receiving yards. Those were the top two receiving seasons in NFL history. Stafford was the quarterback for both players.

Stafford leads the Rams to a thrilling victory against the San Francisco 49ers.

After that, it was on to the Super Bowl. Stafford led the winning drive and became a champion. It was an amazing way to start a new chapter in his career. Rams fans hoped there would be even more to come.

MATTHEW STAFFORD

- Height: 6 feet 3 inches (190 cm)
- Weight: 220 pounds (100 kg)
- Birth date: February 7, 1988
- Birthplace: Tampa, Florida
- High school: Highland Park High School (University Park, Texas)
- College: University of Georgia (Athens, Georgia) (2006–08)
- NFL teams: Detroit Lions (2009–20); Los Angeles Rams (2021–)
- Major awards and championships: NCAA First-Team All-American (2008); NFL Comeback Player of the Year (2011); Pro Bowl (2014); Super Bowl champion (2021)

Detroit

Los Angeles

Athens

University
Park

Tampa

MATTHEW STAFFORD

Write your answers on a separate piece of paper.

1. Write a paragraph that describes the main ideas of Chapter 3.

2. Quarterbacks often get much of the credit or blame for a team's success or failure. Do you think that's fair? Why or why not?

3. In the 2021 season, which team did the Rams play in the first round of the playoffs?

> **A.** Cincinnati Bengals
> **B.** Tampa Bay Buccaneers
> **C.** Arizona Cardinals

4. Why was Stafford the top pick in the 2009 NFL Draft?

> **A.** He graduated from high school early.
> **B.** He had a strong, accurate arm.
> **C.** He threw a lot of interceptions.

Answer key on page 32.

GLOSSARY

backup
A player who does not start the game.

draft
A system that allows teams to acquire new players coming into a league.

durable
Able to deal with minor injuries and keep playing over a long period.

prospect
A player who is likely to be successful in the future.

rookie
A professional athlete in his or her first year.

roster
The list of players on a team.

starter
A player who participates in a game from its beginning.

tumor
A growth of abnormal tissue in the body.

upset
When a team wins a game that it was expected to lose.

TO LEARN MORE

BOOKS

Bowker, Paul. *Best Super Bowl Quarterbacks*. Mankato, MN: 12-Story Library, 2019.

Gitlin, Marty. *The Greatest Quarterbacks of All Time*. San Diego: ReferencePoint Press, 2021.

Hustad, Douglas. *Innovations in Football*. Minneapolis: Abdo Publishing, 2022.

NOTE TO EDUCATORS

Visit **www.focusreaders.com** to find lesson plans, activities, links, and other resources related to this title.

INDEX

Answer Key: 1. Answers will vary; 2. Answers will vary; 3. C; 4. B